Breaking the Silence

Love Doesn't Hurt

By Ikea Clinton

ISBN:978-0-57865845-2

Breaking the Silence (Love Doesn't Hurt)

This is a dedication to the ones parting from such a horrific way of living. To many beautiful women that lost their lives in such a distraught way. Also, for all women going through this hoping that they can get out to share their story and help prevent a lifestyle that is so gruesome.

Tables of Content

Love does a lot of things but one thing it doesn't do is hurt. Love isn't easy, it may cause frustration and growing pains, but it should never hurt. You should never feel that your soul is deteriorating because of the actions of someone else. You and your lover will have your differences but using love and respect as factors to overcome the hard times should make the boundaries nice and clear.

Physical, mental and emotional abuse is committed by people who feel like they own you, who sees you as property. That's not love, that's slavery. We are losing a lot of women through domestic violence. Loving someone that doesn't love you means that you don't love yourself and if that's the case we need to work on that. Imagine sitting in front of your abuser crying your eyes out wanting their sympathy. You want them to look into your eyes and see how much they have hurt you, yet they look into your eyes and show you how much they don't care. They continue to hurt you and put you through pain. Women are so undervalued today. Remember that experiencing a free mind, body and soul is the definition of living life to the fullest. Don't ever let anyone restrain you from your freedom.

My testimony

I and my abuser's relationship started with us being friends. Within time we began to get intimate. The beginning months of our relationship was amazing until I found out he was cheating. The first time my abuser hit me he had punched me in the face because I wanted to break up with him due to his infidelity. (I never experienced someone I genuinely love to hurt me in such a physical way.) I told anyone who asked me about my bruise that I got bit by a spider. My mom took me to the hospital where they prescribed me medicine for my black eye. I consumed the pill as if I did get bit by a spider. I started believing that that was what really happened. I devalued the seriousness in the situation and took him back. He treated me good for months, but his abusive ways continued. Dealing with a lot of mental and physical abuse instead of leaving I began to defend myself and fight back. When I started to protect myself, I became the cause of our household issues, that's what abusers do. In their story you will always be the problem.

The day I realized that I was mentally done from this relationship was the night we fought outside in our car. I didn't attempt to fight him back this time. The argument caught me off guard. I thought we were doing good. Hours past of verbal and physical abuse until daybreak. At this point, it was time for him to go to work. I drove him there and he asked me to wait. He was making up with me at this time. He came out with flowers. I accepted them. I went home and looked at them for a while. I then realized that the flowers were dying. Nine hours before receiving those flowers I read a poem "I got flowers today". After that day I lost all the love that I had for my abuser. My soul felt dead. I had this negative feeling that death was approaching me soon and it lasted for months. After a while, I was just continuing this relationship for this family image I painted in my mind. That is something I had to get the courage to part ways from. I'm here to give you my story and explain how I left this horrible nightmare. This is my testimony something I share so you, my readers understand that this is all coming from experience. These events are based on what I went through, how I left and got out. With putting our voices together, we can start our journey of "Breaking the Silence."

My Last Encounter with My Abuser.

I get to my apartment and I knocked on the door. I banged on the living room window. I knocked on my daughter's window... Nothing... Sick, tired and pregnant I was determined to get inside my house. I broke my screen in my living room to lift the window open. There he is drunk and passed out. I threw all the items I had on me at him hoping that I will hit him and that he might wake up but again nothing. I yell for my daughter; she eventually comes out in the outfit she had worn throughout the day the house looks distraught as if she had been up by herself for hours. Hi mommy she says relieved to see me. Hey baby, I try and share nothing but calm energy with her. Wake up your dad I tell her. I stepped on the outside piece of my living room A.C. I climbed inside the window my bottom is on the barrier and there is one leg in the house and one outside now stuck in this position I'm in pain crying and screaming at the top of my lungs. He finally got up as he staggered to me completely incoherent. I push him away hoping he can get out of his dazed mind state.... His body comes back to me. I push him again he wakes up angry. As I am stuck in the window hoping he'll be able to help me soon I see a faded image of my daughter and she look so stunned. Completely losing myself with sadness. Hurt that this is still my life, my reality. It's one else's but mine. If only I would have taken my key. This would have all ended differently.

He charges at me with full force my movement is to slow when he approaches me with a blow. One after another constantly coming at me. He's too strong for me to take on at that moment. I'm losing the baby I yell.... I'm having a miscarriage please stop. My daughter's presence is no longer visible to me. I know if he gets me in this house at this moment, he most likely will kill me. I won't be able to fight back being that I can barely hold myself together now. He's gripping my body as I grab on to my neighbor's balcony he grabbed my leg and began to bite on it I start to kick with my free leg as I hold on to the bar of the balcony above. I knock him off my leg I jump down to land on the grass in front of my apartment than ran... Good thing I did because out the door he came. As I continuously ran, I lost him I stopped to catch my breath this guy walking looked at me and seen that I was hysterical. He stopped and asked me if I was okay. I'm fine I stated. He stared at me skeptically and he proceeded on his way. The keys to my vehicle are in the house along with my phone. I had to go back to get my daughter and get out of there.

I look inside my apartment through the opened window I don't see my daughter... And he looks calm, I go inside to face my penalty. The second he sees me he started ranting you're a bitch, a slut, a whore... Sit your ass down. I see my keys and glanced at my daughter as she's in the corner of the living room there is no way I can grab my keys my kid and get to the car. As my only plan to escape goes down the drain in front of my eyes I know the only thing I can do is to stay there and try to keep him calm until I can escape. He steps into my kitchen while he's in there I grab my phone and sit on top of it. I heard a beer can open I pulled my phone and text my sister... "Can you come and get me." I then delete the text out of my phone so there would be no proof of my only way out. Just trying to avoid him breaking my phone into pieces this time around... I'm holding my daughter crying... He comes out of the kitchen with a knife. He looks at me in disgust and he begins to cry... He cuts his arm until the white meat was exposed like an over cooked hot dog. You see what you do to me he said as he puts the knife down and begins to hit me... My daughter chimes in... And says daddy you don't hit mommy... You don't hurt mommy... Say Sorry! He looked at her and chuckled... I learned after the first time he held me hostage is not to cry... He doesn't care and not to scream because no one else cares either. I have a bite mark on my leg and hand there both black and blue. He hits me again in the face as he rants on, I hold my daughter. Crying kissing her in so much sorrow that due to my stupidity I'm in this predicament again. In my thoughts making promises that I don't know if I would be able to keep. Held hostage in my own house. After time the monster fell asleep as well did I. It took me some time, but I was ready. I gained some strength and he was going to hear my raft in the morning.

Left for Dead

My mind is being controlled by possession

It's no longer mines.

My soul is being snatched outta my body

I'm not gonna get it back this time.

Being obedient today isn't gonna keep me alive.

I'm dead and gone, it's too late to be revived.

The bruises on my body doesn't have any comparison to the damage done inside.

The water that fed my fruitfulness has been replaced with poison and I'm sun deprived.

My emotions are overwhelmed with pain, hurt, and fear.

I'm so fragile I know my dead soul can't be repaired.

My life dwindles every minute as my body lays here on the floor.

As I fade away, I hear him exit out the door.

Here I am left for dead.

I knew today I should have escaped instead.

We as women, the most **POWERFUL** creatures on this earth must know when we're being treated wrong. Domestic violence is an unfortunate repeating cycle. This is the **BLUEPRINT** we are giving our loved ones to follow by living in such an environment. **ENERGY** is transferable so the surroundings you and your loved ones are around has a significant role in your life. They're will be people that will help encourage you to leave and others may sit and watch but it's solely your **RESPONSIBILITY** to leave such a dangerous lifestyle while you still have the option to. We as women must know our worth. No woman should be **LEFT FOR DEAD**, but sadly there is an excessive amount that has been.

His Game

As I enter the room it looks so appealing.

A shiny marble floor and chandeliers on the ceiling.

A candle lit dinner with

a gift box on the side.

Over filled with joy as tears ran down my eyes.

Here he comes right behind me with a dozen of roses.

I embrace the roses with my eyes closed to smell the scent

Click clack is what I hear as the Glock resets.

Am I going to make it to the end of the day?

Or is my life going to be taken in a gruesome way.

I ball into a corner as that's my method of self-defense.

Today as I sit here in this corner, I realize my life is compromisable at his dispense.

I hear the gun hesitate 3 times than released on the 4th.

I clinch my body as I hear the bullet penetrate the floor.

He giggles than laugh with a sigh.

You lived today but remember your life is mine.

This is the game you have **ENTERED**. His personal game of **RUSSIAN ROULETTE**. You don't know what day will be your last. The ball is in his court. You're a sitting **DUCK** in your own life. You've allowed someone one else to have more control than you do. You have **SURRENDERED** your life, dignity, happiness and freedom. Is this how you imagine life being?

Given Strength

Daddy don't hit my mommy that's not nice

Is what destroyed my brain.

My child is the number one witness of my pain.

Hearing her cry of my physical image.

The safety net I try and provide for my baby has diminished.

You would think with her voice he'd slow down.

Hearing my little girls cry was a hurtful sound.

I stood up with a power I didn't know I had.

I took our daughter and put her behind me.

His face filled with confusion.

He didn't know what I was doing.

But I charged at him with full force.

Begin to hit him with no remorse.

A kick to the penis,

And a hit to his head

I knew if we didn't get away that I would be dead.

While he tries to grasp his composure

I pick up my baby and ran for dear life.

My freedom and my daughter are worth the risk and sacrifice.

In the middle of winter holding her running down the street.

Me and my baby deserve to be free.

The strength your child can give you is amazing. I know only because my children give me an **UNREMARKABLE** amount of strength. My daughter gave me the strength to stay in an abusive relationship as well as get **OUT**. Our first instinct as mothers is to always **PROTECT** our children that's our job. When I dealt with abuse during my pregnancy from then on, I seen how much **STRENGTH** I withheld. I remember the day I picked my baby up and ran for dear life as the jogging became **ENDLESS,** we made it to our destination. My daughter seeing me getting abused by her father affected her more than I knew. I began to see it in her actions, the way she interacts with people I see how much harm was done to her **MENTALLY**. As I'm here trying to help heal her distraught emotions, I will never make the decision to stay in something so traumatizing because of the effect it has on my mental health as well as my kids. We as women provide so much **NURTURE** to our families. I thought holding on to the relationship with my children's father would be best for the kids even though I mentally left it years ago. It's understandable to want to make your family work. But it's not okay to put you and your children in harm's way because of it.

Enough

My pain his power

I sit on the floor in front of him looking at his strength.

With my black eye, I try to determine if the door was arm's length.

It wasn't a good day. Today I locked the bathroom door.

I walk out to greet him with one blow I was on the floor.

Should I fight back?

I realize there's no winning simply because he's sober.

Should I make a run for it or take this beating.

Today is the day that I finally say I'm leaving.

He puts his hand back for another blow.

Never in my life have I felt so low.

He points to the bathroom and says this is my house you leave all doors open.

I'm so sorry baby I say loving hiding all emotions.

He went in the room with his case of beer.

I stayed right there in that corner in pain full of fear.

I cried and cried with the thought of what to do.

I was emotionally exhausted and physically through.

I went and laid in the bed hearing me cry he decided to turn over.

My cry didn't affect him from having his way.

His abusive tactics in the bedroom are generally the same.

He pins my arms down and shoves himself inside of me till I moan in pain.

He kisses my deformed body with so much gentleness.

How can he hurt me so much than treat me with care?

He chokes me as he begins to cum.

I'm happy this is over he's almost done.

He cuddles me tight and that soothes him to sleep.

I wait for him to knock out as I weep.

I ease out of his restrainment quickly and quietly packed my stuff.

I know this is gonna be tough

But today is the day I said I had enough.

Today is the day you said I've had **ENOUGH**. Today is the day you say I love myself way too much to be treated like this. Today is the day you say I'm going to leave because I have that option. Abuse comes in so many different forms such as **SEXUAL, MENTAL, EMOTIONAL, AND PHYSICAL**. The abuse will not stop once the disrespect has been done and your abuser sees that you allowed it by staying or coming back, they will continue. Do not tolerate **DISRESPECT** on any level. The relationship that you have with yourself reflects on what you will **ACCEPT** from a relationship with your lover.

Love Bandit

I took your heart without permission.

When it wasn't mine to take.

I didn't care about the condition.

Fondling with it whether it would break.

It's mine so I do what I please.

My happiness inflates by preying on you.

The heart I have is stuck in an ice box, and there is where it will freeze.

I need yours so I can use it till it cease.

Once I've used it all up, I'll give it back to you.

Then I would have to let it go and attract something new.

This is the way I live I'm not saying it's normal.

In my world I put nothing on the line for me to lose.

My life is filled of victory.

Your happiness is because of me.

Something is wrong because I blend in with everyone else.

I'm oblivious to my imbalanced emotions itself.

But you are now abandoned.

Because you are a victim of the love bandit.

The **LOVE BANDIT** has came and turned your world upside down. He took your **HEART** and fed on it till it's ceased. Now here you are without the most important **ORGAN** in your body. What do you do now?

Your forced to **LIVE** and continue life without it? All because you **WILLINGLY** gave someone else to much. It's okay to give but you must make sure you have enough to **NURTURE** yourself so you can continue to give to those who deserve the best and healthiest part of you.

A Woman Lost

I left

Damaged but I left.

My body will heal in time.

I can't say the same for my mind.

Leaving him was the hardest.

Living under the mind control of a con artist.

The first 2 weeks I wanted to go back desperately.

He loves me he didn't mean to hurt me I'm sure of it.

This is what I would say to myself. When he didn't care about me not one bit.

I'm shaking, scratching, and can't hold any food down.

I was so dependent on that relationship but I'm going cold turkey without it now.

Scared to be in my thoughts scared about my surroundings.

I feel as if I have no worth without him.

Being in my skin is so discouraging and shameful.

My family is concerned with the choices I've been making.

Love was my choice of drug I didn't think it was this strong, but I was sadly mistaken.

As each day goes by life begins to feel a little easier

I had to pick out of being a battered female or a dead woman I picked neither.

LOST without your abuser? Good, it's good that you feel this way. Congratulations you're finally free. Yes, living in this world and it's just you now. The same feeling you felt when you **BROKE LOOSE** from your parents or caretakers. Just that your leaving someone that try and control your **GREATNESS**. They tried and dim the beauty you have. It's okay to be lost you're a step closer from finding yourself. This part is the hardest step, but you will overcome this like the **WONDERFUL WOMAN** you are! The hardest part is leaving.... Building the courage to leave can take years, some people don't make it out at all unfortunately. You go through so many different emotions. Should I leave? Am I the problem? How can I make this relationship better? You should leave while you can. No, you're not the problem. And you can't make it better. You're going to leave and want to go back.... He is going to try to convince to come back. He's going to say he can't live without you. He's **OBSESSED** with the power he has over you. The control! Someone with such **MENTAL INSTABILITY** needs to work on themselves. You must truly want the change for yourself for your leaving to be successful. There is a possibility that you may go thru withdrawal but you're just going must stay strong emotionally. Your life's going to just have to be a **PRIORITY** for you at this time to get through this phase.

Not Worthy of Love

I don't deserve to be loved.

I'm not pretty,

I'm not smart.

No one would want me,

No one would love me.

I come from nothing,

I have nothing to give.

If you haven't got the point

I'm worthless.

The person I am completely torn down.

From inside out.

The physical abuse my body would heal itself within days

But my thoughts I live in its something that doesn't easily go away.

I got this drilled into my head day and night

For 6 years.

That's how I truly feel about myself

I don't want anyone's love.

I don't want my own.

Simply because I don't deserve to be loved.

You're going to go through times where you feel **UNWORTHY** and beneath yourself. That happens especially being a victim of mental abuse. But I'm telling you to look in the mirror **EMBRACE** yourself. Say this is me the **NATURAL** me, the **PURE** me love yourself. That will be the only way you will be blessed with **TRUE LOVE** is if you find it within yourself.

Your Story

You are amazing I love you...

You are amazing I love you.

You made it through.

You're no longer a victim of abuse.

You value yourself or your loved ones more than the person sucking out your liveliness.

You overcame his soul diminishing death wish.

What you've been through is going to stick with you for infinity and beyond.

But remember life depends on the way you respond.

You write your story.

As it is yours to write.

This isn't a game because what you are living is your life.

You are amazing. Your beautiful. You're going through an internal **CLEANSING PROCESS**. This world has so many amazing things to offer. There's great people and **MESMERIZING** places. Don't limit yourself to something that's gonna do nothing but hurt you in the end... Don't dim your light for no one. It's time to smile and laugh at the **BEAUTY** in this world. Experience life the best way you can remember *"You die once but you have the option to live everyday"* embrace that because this is **YOUR STORY**.

The Lotus Flower

I grew.

I'm growing.

Without my abuser.

I slowly rised above the mud I knew was weighing me down.

Stainless and beautiful like a cleaned crown.

I look down and see the layers of dirt and mud that I rised above.

Never did I think I would make it here.

Enjoying the beauty of the sun.

The warmth of nature.

The breezed provide by oxygen.

I'm alive and I made it.

From one healing soul to another, KNOW YOUR WORTH!

This here is my story and for anyone living this man or woman. The best advice I can give you is to leave. Dismantle this lifestyle while you still have the option to. Free yourself from the pain and misery with any toxic relationship you are holding on to by walking away. One out of every three person has been a victim of domestic violence.

Breaking the cycle

Cycle of abuse
- ⬜ Love and kindness
- ⬜ Power gain through isolation
- ⬜ Restriction of activities
- ⬜ Punishment (verbal or physical harm)
- ⬜ Acting as if nothing ever happened

www.ingramcontent.com/pod-product-compliance
Lightning Source LLC
Chambersburg PA
CBHW081159090426
42736CB00017B/3393